SAGAN UM TÖLURNAR

THE NUMBER STORY

SMALL BOOK ONE

ENGLISH - ICELANDIC

Numbers Teach Children
Their Number Names

written and illustrated by

MISS ANNA

Early Reader Edition of *The Number Story 1*
Bronze Medal Winner, 2016 Wishing Shelf Book Award

Lumpy Publishing

Cover by | Lumpy Publishing
Layout by | Lumpy Publishing
Translated by Sigurlaug Valdimarsdottir
Coloring by Jieeun Woo and Maria Mirabella

Library of Congress Control Number: 2018902040

Names: Miss Anna, author.
Title: Number story : numbers teach children their number names / Miss Anna.
Description: Portland, OR: Lumpy Publishing, 2018.
Identifiers: ISBN 978-1-945977-47-3 | LCCN 2018902040
Summary: The pictures and rhymes present stories which introduce numbers 0-10.
Subjects: LCSH Numeration—English--Icelandic--Pictorial works--Juvenile literature. | BISAC JUVENILE NONFICTION /
Languages: English--Icelandic
Classification: LCC QA141.3 .M57 2018 | DDC 513—dc23

Publisher: Lumpy Publishing
Website: www.missannabooks.com
Email: missanna@missannabooks.com

Paperback: ISBN 978-1-945977-47-3
Printed in the U.S.A.   1 3 5 7 9 10 8 6 4 2

Viltu læra
hvað tölurnar heita?

It is very easy and a lot of fun!

Það er mjög auðvelt og mikið gaman!

Say-along our little jingle

Syngdu með laginu

starting from Number One!

Byrjum á númer eitt!

1

ONE looks like my one finger.

EINN

lítur út eins og einn
fingurinn minn.

1
ONE!
EINN!

2

TWO trails a tail.

TVEIR

er með skott.

A TAIL! SKOTT!

3

THREE has bumps.

ÞRÍR

hefur hóla.

BUMPY! HÓLAR!

4

FOUR carries a sail.

FJÓRIR

er með segl.

4
A SAIL!
SEGL!

5

FIVE   is a racing track.

FIMM

er kappakstursbraut.

VROOM
BRÚÚMM !

SIX   curves like a snail.

SEX

beygist eins og snigill.

A SNAIL!   SNIGILL!

7

SEVEN has a sharp angle.

SJÖ

er með beitt horn.

OUCH!
ÁI!

8

EIGHT is rollercoaster rails.

ÁTTA

er rússíbani.

JIBBÍ!
YIPPEE!

NINE   is a bubble on a stick.

NÍU

er að blása sápukúlur.

A BUBBLE! SÁPUKÚLA!

10

TEN   is an eye of a whale.

TÍU

er eitt auga á hvali.

WINK!
BLIKK!
HELLO! HALLÓ!

And
Og

0

ZERO   is an empty pail.

NÚLL

er tóm fata.

IT'S EMPTY!
Hún er tóm!

Thank you for playing with us today.

We had a lot of fun too!

Takk fyrir að leika með okkur í dag.

Við skemmtum okkur líka vel!

We are your Number friends,
Zero to Ten,
Who will be here for you~
Við erum tölu vinirnir nýju
Frá núll til tíu!
Við verðum hér fyrir þig~

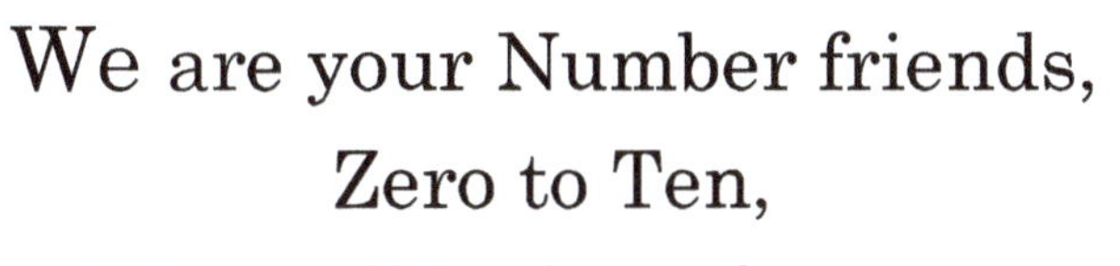

Bye-bye now!
See you again soon!
Bæ bæ núna!
Sjáumst fljótt aftur!

The Numbers are *SINGING* too!

To sing-a-long, look for Miss Anna Number Story
at your favorite music store like iTUNES.

MP3

| Numbers 0-10 IDENTIFYING & COUNTING | Numbers 11-20 & Ordinals first, second, third... | Numbers 0-100 & Place Values ones, tens, hundreds... | About Clocks & Telling Time hours, minutes, seconds |

Number Story 1 & 2

isbn: 978-0-996216-48-7

Number Story 3 & 4

isbn: 978-1-945977-01-5

Number Story 5 & 6

isbn: 978-1-945977-06-0

Number Story 7 & 8

isbn: 978-1-949320-40-4

For more Miss Anna books to love,
visit us at

www.missannabooks.com

Numbers are working hard all over the world!
Come Travel the World with Us!

9 781945 977473